Brok

Also by Chris Highland

Meditations of John Muir
Nature's Temple

A Freethinker's Gospel
Essays for a Sacred Secular World

My Address Is a River
A Place to Belong, Closer to Home

Life After Faith
Radical Paths to a Reasonable Spirituality

Meditations of John Burroughs
Nature Is Home

Meditations of Margaret Fuller
The Inner Stream

Meditations of Henry David Thoreau
A Light in the Woods

You can contact Chris Highland on his website,
chighland.com, where he shares insights for
personal growth.

Broken Bridges

Building Community in a World Divided by Beliefs

Chris Highland

INSIGHTING GROWTH
Publications Inc.

Broken Bridges: Building Community in a World Divided by Beliefs

Cover Photo by Chris Highland

Chris Highland
www.chighland.com

Printed in the United States of America

First Edition: June 2020

Insighting Growth Publications
Houston, Texas
www.IGrowPub.com

ISBN-13: 978-1-7333520-6-2 (Paperback)
ISBN-13: 978-1-7333520-7-9 (Kindle Edition)

"Your ancient ruins shall be rebuilt; you shall raise up the foundations of many generations; you shall be called the repairer of the breach, the restorer of streets to live in."

Isaiah 58:12 NRSV

About the Author

Chris Highland was born and raised in the Pacific Northwest and lived for over 35 years in the San Francisco Bay Area. He was a Protestant minister and Interfaith chaplain for many years before becoming a Humanist celebrant.

Chris earned a degree in Religion and Philosophy from Seattle Pacific University, an evangelical Christian school. He received a Master of Divinity degree from San Francisco Theological Seminary, a member of the Graduate Theological Union in Berkeley, California. He has been active in "presence ministry"—being present with people experiencing brokenness—in a private school, county jails, among homeless people, as well as directing an emergency shelter, and managing affordable housing for seniors.

He is the author of a dozen books including *A Freethinker's Gospel*, *Meditations of John Muir*, *My Address is a River*, and other books. Chris has taught courses on Nature literature and Freethought in California and North Carolina.

Since 2016 he has been writing weekly "Highland Views" columns for the *Asheville Citizen-Times*, a USA Today affiliate, addressing an array of issues concerning faith and secularism.

Chris and his wife Carol, a Presbyterian minister, live on the edge of the Blue Ridge Mountains in Asheville, North Carolina.

Contents

Introduction.. 1

To the Bridge... 7

States of Mind.. 11

Inter-Marriage 17

We/They... 21

Frederick Douglass 25

Native Drums.. 31

Radical Presence 35

Secular Blessings... 39

Angels Aware.. 45

Made for Cooperation 49

Tribal Nature.. 53

Dismantling Fences 57

Open Tables.. 61

Higher Ethics... 65

Risky Trust 69

Extinguish Evil 73

Faith in Questions 79

Repairing Brokenness.....................................83

Better than Unity 87

3 C's..91

Colors of Truth..97

Healthier Choices..101

Reader Response 105

Endnotes 106

To Benny

and others who repair

the brokenness

Introduction

Thomas, a young Ethiopian man, found me through my nature writings. After sending him several of my books and a pair of binoculars for his birdwatching, we began an exchange of emails. Thomas sends beautiful images of his country often accompanied by perceptive comments and questions.

In one email, Thomas was deeply troubled by the violence on the streets of America. He wrote, "What is behind all this brutality?" He had other questions. "Who is responsible for being human?" And with race, ethnicity, and selfishness on his mind, he asked, "What makes us a special one in the face of Nature?"

Thomas never fails to give me something to think about. Our common concern for the natural world and shared disturbance at the injustices in Africa and America, serve as bridges across the cultures, nationalities, and ocean that separate us.

At times it seems there are too many broken bridges in our world—all the shattered and splintered divisions my young African friend sees and feels deeply. How could we ever begin to repair, restore or replace them? And there are so many places where no bridges ever existed. Where do we begin? What tools do we have? How do we even find the language to work alongside other builders?

A college professor in New York wrote: "I often feel that my primary role is to give [students] a vocabulary to think about—and put into words—what they already know."[1] We know more than we think. We may simply need a teacher to give us a framework, sturdy words to use as tools to build our foundation of knowledge. Our teachers won't always have college degrees, yet they can help us find the materials to repair what is broken or build what has never been.

In college, I was emerging from a very narrow worldview. Life was a gully rather than the Grand Canyon, and Jesus was my only "bridge over troubled waters." Coming out of a deeply emotional, Bible-based, evangelical culture, I was now confronted with using my mind in uncomfortable ways. Questions rattled my brain like earthquakes. As one restricted world crumbled, a wider world came into view. My mind was expanding, beginning to span the divides, which were primarily gaps in my reasoning.

Courses in World Religions through college and seminary further encouraged me to make connections where there were major disconnects within and between faith traditions. A major reason I chose chaplaincy as my career was the multi-faith nature of the work. With a workable knowledge of the beliefs, practices and vocabulary of various religions, I felt better equipped to be effective as a chaplain representing an array of faith perspectives.

As the professor in New York senses, I often feel that my years of ministry and my current teaching and writing share that same primary goal—to help people find the words to express what they already know. Like the student who told me after a class on Freethought I was teaching: "I never knew I was a 'freethinker'—thank you for giving me a word that describes me."

Unless we are content to listen only to our own echo in the canyon, our curiosity may lead us to ask ourselves bridging questions: Do I know one of "them"? Have I met the "other" on the "other side"? Think of someone you hear or read about but have never met. Who are they? Could you learn more about yourself by knowing them? Asking the uncomfortable questions of ourselves is the only way to start the great collapse, crumbling the old to build the new, or use lumber that was once a wall to build a door or a bridge that lasts.

Religious faith often defends the crumbling spans and cracked walls of the past (while chipping away at important barriers like the wall of separation between religion and state). There can be resistance to repairing the breaches. The voices of prophets who spoke truth to their age are often forgotten. Over my years of interfaith work, I heard some of those voices, many in unexpected places like jail cells, homeless camps, and mental health facilities. I was privileged to meet people in the middle of many bridges, often during transitions in their lives. And sometimes I stood with people in the wreckage of the overpass they once thought was stable.

This book is an invitation to repair, when we can, and to be honest when there are irreparable obstacles. We'll only know what is possible when we stand together and face the gaps and gulfs, then try to find the best crossings and gather needed tools and materials. We have to ask ourselves: What's the purpose of our cooperative construction? How will we do it? Is it even possible to create the crossings? Who will risk the long walk over?

In these pages you will meet many risk-takers, each restoring hope for themselves and for their world. Benny goes to the Golden Gate Bridge one night, intent on jumping. Frederick Douglass articulates things we already know about injustice. We hear the voices of repairers and reformers who walk the rough and ragged edges of faith communities: Buddhist, Jewish, Muslim, Native American, and Progressive Christian. More secular calls ring out from The Dalai Lama, John Burroughs, Terry Tempest Williams, and others who lift up the voices of the natural world.

Obstacles remain. Some bridges are so badly damaged they may need to be abandoned to search for another way. No one has a lock on the truth. Said another way, no one can completely dismantle the bridges that unite the human species, and no person, tradition, or power has a right to set barriers in the way of free access to a better place.

The questions Thomas asked echo across the wide divide: "Who is responsible for being human?" "What is behind all this brutality?" "What makes us a special one in the face of Nature?"

To begin to respond to these challenging questions, we must be willing to "pair up" and repair together. Where there is brokenness, it is up to us to restore. There is no manual, no "how to" book to carry along. If this book suggests anything new, it's probably something we already know.

Some of us have a fear of heights. My wife gets anxious walking across some bridges. There is actually a medical condition called "Gephyrophobia" defined as: "An abnormal and persistent fear of crossing bridges. Sufferers of this phobia experience undue anxiety even though they realize their fear is irrational."[2]

If you experience gephyrophobia while reading the pages that follow, take heart. You're not alone.

Chris Highland

To the Bridge

Benny was an older gentleman who would drop into the chaplaincy office now and then. Sometimes, my assistant Elizabeth and I would be working on a project or handling someone's "issue" and turn around to see Benny sitting, silent and patient. Usually, Benny had a smile on his face, a bit like a Cheshire cat. Or, he would look a bit lost. In any case, we would welcome Benny and ask what he was up to.

For a period of time, Benny was without a permanent dwelling, a state sometimes referred to as "homeless." When he finally got into an apartment he could afford with social security and his veteran's pension, he was thrilled. Now and again, he would show up when we would pick up people at the St. Vincent's free dining room downtown for one of our "outings"—a van trip to a lake, forest, or beach.

Benny seemed to prefer being a loner, yet, he kept showing up.

One day Benny found me in the office. He looked troubled. "What's on your mind?" I asked.

"I went to the bridge last night," he shrugged.

"What does that mean?" I asked.

"I just felt bad and didn't think I could take this anymore," he confessed. "I took a bus to the bridge [the Golden Gate Bridge] and walked across. For some reason, I decided not to jump. I don't know why."

I listened closely, as chaplains do. I said, "Well, Benny, you knew some of us would miss you, and we'd be angry with you too!" He smiled. We laughed.

From then on, whenever Benny appeared, I assumed he needed the companionship. Or he simply didn't want to be alone. I suppose that's the same thing.

At the end of some months, low on cash, he would ask me for a few dollars. He always paid me back.

There were times when I noticed Benny giving an encouraging word to another person who was feeling low. To me, this was evidence of something we often said: Anyone can serve as a chaplain.

One afternoon I came into our office and found a note from Benny. "I'm going to the bridge. Thank you for everything."

I quickly drove across town to the lounge where Benny hung out. Benny was sitting at the bar and turned to see me walk in—almost as if he expected me. I sat with him, ordered a brew, and let him talk.

Benny decided not to go to the bridge.

People who are suicidal are in deep emotional pain and are often crying out for someone to notice, to care, to just be with them. Despair is a slippery, muddy trail in a dark forest. At times, the best another person can do is walk along that trail for a short time with a person who is suffering. It's not about rescuing, though there are times when we need rescuing—when the house, or the heart, is in flames. There's tremendous power in one human being finding time, making time, to "be human" with another human being.

Religious faith can help some people through these dark times. Yet, in my experience, it's critically important to assist the hopeless person to find something hopeful, to have faith in themselves, assuring them we have faith in them too.

Benny stood in the chaplaincy doorway one afternoon with a piece of paper in his hand. He'd been observing how the chaplain team was encouraging and promoting the music of the streets. We had produced an album of original music to raise awareness of the talent of unhoused people and to raise much-needed funds for the chaplaincy.

Benny handed the paper to me. "Maybe you can make a song out of this."

I read the words he had scribbled on the page.

> You need to forgive all your sadness and your sorrow.

You need to forget the past and look into tomorrow.

I love this great big beautiful world.

And I thank God that I'm alive!

I sat down with a guitar and tried a few tunes with his lyrics. Benny sat across from me with a big smile on his face. We knew how significant those words were.

A few months later, I took some of our musicians to a local congregation to play their original "songs of the street." I gave the morning message. Then, we led the congregation in singing Benny's song: "The World is Mine." He wasn't there that morning. He was probably in one of his "funk" moods or maybe at a casino or his bar. I don't know if that congregation could fully appreciate his gift that morning, but everyone seemed to love the song.

I wonder if some of the most meaningful gifts are those given out of hopelessness, instability, and uncertainty. I wonder if there are amazing ideas and solutions to community issues, just waiting to be heard by anyone who might give some time to listen. Truthfully, I don't wonder about that. Benny taught me how true it can be.

Benny took a leap, but it was toward building something better for himself and for others. Through his presence and his music, Benny joined the growing community of bridge builders.

States of Mind

My wife Carol and I took a month to drive across the country while moving from California to North Carolina. It was our own risky leap into the unknown, leaving stable jobs and deep roots in the Bay Area. Yet, Carol's elderly mother was alone, and we felt the need to be nearer.

Crossing over border after border from city to city, in a land divided in myriad ways, we passed through a total of twelve states. In our own "states of mind" we made the journey an adventure, driven by the intention of learning more of both history and nature.

Hikes in Glacier and Yellowstone National Parks were balanced by powerful hours of learning at the George Washington Carver National Monument in Diamond, Missouri, the Brown vs. Board of Education National Historical Site in Topeka, Kansas, the John Brown Memorial Park in Osawatomie, Kansas, and the National Civil Rights Museum at the Lorraine Motel in Memphis, Tennessee.

Mile after mile, bridge after bridge, through mountains, prairies, and pastureland, we felt immersed in this incredibly diverse patch of earth known as the U.S.A. This was no "vacation," it was an education, a kind of secular pilgrimage.

Now living in North Carolina, we continue our explorations deeper into the South. History and Nature keep calling us.

I had never been to Chattanooga, Tennessee, or anywhere in Alabama, with only a brief visit to Savannah, Georgia, so our next journey was educational in significant ways. It may sound like a travel-log, but buckle up, and I'll show you where this is going.

In some ways, my wife and I are typical travelers. We love the experience of seeing new places, meeting locals, and trying the food and brews. The natural beauty that recognizes no state boundaries calls to us, making us feel each state is our land too. We're more than tourists— we're on a class field trip, and the whole country is the school.

Apart from the places, people, and parks, it's the history that draws us to go deeper. What happened here, and why? The lessons pour in like the flash and rumble of those southern rainstorms.

Images from the highway: paved pathways through tunnels of trees; rolling green hills and fields of crops; cloudbursts that force you to pull off the road; "historic" towns beckoning for tourist dollars; endless strings of trucks full of "essential stuff"; a "War on Terror Highway" sign; a massive rebel flag; JESUS billboards; cross after cross after cross; welcoming rest stops to stretch weary legs and soothe tired eyes.

Chattanooga took us right up Lookout Mountain. A good symbol for what we like: a bit of history and a beautiful view. Chattanooga is a sensual city shaped by the snaking Tennessee River. With emotion, we stood where Cherokee families were gathered for "removal and relocation."

On an evening crossing of Chickamauga Lake, we saw osprey, leaping bass, and a stunning sunset. Just over the Georgia border, a visit to the Chickamauga battlefield gave us more context for the Blue and the Gray.

In Dayton, Tennessee, we stood in the courtroom where a young teacher was defended by Clarence Darrow during the famous "monkey trial." Thinking about what happened there made me wonder how much we've actually evolved.

Birmingham, Alabama, was where we began to see more clearly how religion can fuel either hatred or hope. Standing at the top of the huge iron statue of the god Vulcan overlooking the city, we could see where the fire of creative industry meets the destructive flames of injustice.

Birmingham was once known as "Bombingham" due to the frequent bombings of churches and homes. In the

center of town, Ingram Park offers a beautiful walk
through an ugly part of our history. Images from our
national memory—blasting firehoses and police dogs
attacking non-violent marchers—become flesh and blood
realities.

Adjacent to the park, the National Civil Rights Institute is
a powerful classroom that teaches the stories of our un-
civil wrongs and points to hopeful ways forward. In one
corner, you can stand at a large window that looks across
the street to the 16th Street Baptist Church where four
young black girls were killed in a 1963 bombing. Then,
you can scan over the park to the place where marching
children were met with hoses, clubs, dogs, and handcuffs.

We drove across town to the site where Martin Luther
King, Jr. wrote his famous "Letter from Birmingham City
Jail," a writing I consider a modern-day "secular
scripture."

Our next stop was Montgomery, which became the center
of the civic rights classroom for me. It seemed that each
block told a startling story.

We walked by Martin Luther King, Jr's Dexter Avenue
Baptist Church where marchers from Selma arrived in
1965. We stopped at the Greyhound bus station where
Freedom Riders were met by an enraged white mob.

We stood silent at the site where Rosa Parks stepped up
into a bus, in the same square where slaves stepped up to

be auctioned.

The Peace and Justice Memorial was perhaps the most disturbing experience. You slowly walk down into it and look up at 800 six-foot monuments that symbolize thousands of racial terror lynching victims in the United States. Reading the names, dates, and, in some cases, the reasons these people—black and white—were lynched in counties across the country, leaves one speechless. We observed a young black boy tracing the names with his fingers.

Atlanta was our last major stop. There we visited the King Center, MLK's gravesite, birth home, and the Ebenezer Baptist Church, where we sat to listen to a recording of his first sermon there.

Finally, we swung by Stone Mountain, the Mount Rushmore of the South, a Civil War memorial to Jefferson Davis, Robert E. Lee, and Thomas "Stonewall" Jackson. We were delighted by the waterfalls washing over the sand-blasted figures that mar the natural beauty. We've visited many Civil War sites like this in the South, each one causing deeper reflection on our tragic history of national division. Every battleground is a shrine to brokenness, not simply a call, but a scream to build some kind of bridge to be better Americans, let alone better human beings.

There's much more to see and learn in this expansive classroom and sanctuary called America, and the necessary subject is our deep need to listen for the truth of our shared history and to learn more from each other.

Mindful traveling can help us understand what we need to do as citizens, meeting others who are different, learning more of our common history, and our interwoven nature. What might be possible if we move across the land, in a car or in our minds, risking to cross barriers, beyond the *Our Side/Your Side* boundaries?

What if we remembered what unites us as people, and as a People—We the People?

.

Inter-Marriage

When I met my wife, Carol, we were carrying the cross. Seriously. It was an ecumenical Good Friday service at a large downtown church in San Rafael, California. We joined other ministers in hauling a big cross into the sanctuary before leading the service.

I was about to "follow Jesus out the door" of the Church —and religion—while retaining my position as an interfaith chaplain on the streets. Carol held an advocacy position with a nonprofit organization, working with immigrants from many countries living in a low-income neighborhood. I visited her where she worked, and she came to see my tiny office tucked behind the organ pipes in the same church where we carried the cross.

A mutual respect developed as well as a professional and personal attraction.

Over the next five years, we grew close, lived together for a few years, and in 2005 I moved to a small cabin on an island in Washington state to work the land and write a few books. Carol had taken a new job as the director of an interfaith council with responsibilities that spanned the San Francisco Bay Area.

In 2008, I returned to California to marry Carol at a Zen Buddhist center with celebrant friends who were Buddhist, Jewish, Christian, and Wiccan. Carol's parents, Janet and Charlie, reaffirmed their vows that day. It was their 50th anniversary.

I originally wrote this chapter on my dear wife's 56th birthday. It seemed good then, as it does now, to honor her with a few words, not only because she's my wife, but because her years of service and her exceptional talents deserve recognition. I also think our marriage might offer some insights into the joys and challenges of an inter-faith, inter-secular relationship.

I asked Carol if she could describe a thread, or a stream, that runs through her years of ministry. *"Relationships* and *inclusion* have been central," she said.

> As I reflect upon my life thus far, every chapter is founded upon significant connections with friends, family, colleagues, mentors. They root and ground me as I keep uncovering the depths of who I am.

In terms of inclusivity, she says, "Ever since I can recall, I have had an inner sense of 'knowing' that all persons are invited and included in the great scheme of life."

I asked her to explain how a person of deep faith can live in a committed relationship with someone who doesn't believe the way she does. (I have a certain personal interest in her response.)

> What's important to me is depth and
> authenticity—and commitment to treating all
> sentient beings with respect and dignity.
> Whether or not Chris believes in a Supreme
> Being or the certainty of an afterlife, these are
> not requirements for our relationship to be
> authentic, committed and have depth. His
> beliefs are simply not deal-breakers for the
> love and bond we share.

She went on to say that our common bond is love, respect, joy of the outdoors, family, as well as sharing in a good movie or story, tasty food, and travel.

In other words, keeping life simple in a complex world.

We support each other's gifts and skills, and share a joy in assisting others in meaningful, creative ways. Carol adds, "We also admire in each other the talents we seek to deepen in ourselves—Chris' writing and teaching, Carol's networking and bridge-building." As you can tell, this is all very personal.

Our marriage is far from perfect—whatever a "perfect" relationship is imagined to be. One thing to emphasize is that we do not "tolerate" each other's beliefs or lack of belief. We certainly have disagreements, but we often share similar views of the good and bad in our world.

Though I don't often attend church with her, I do go to hear her speak as a guest minister now and then—I've even been known to read a scripture verse in a service. She has accompanied me to lend support when I lecture or give book readings.

If you are in an inter-faith or inter-secular relationship, it may help to know that, like any marriage, it takes work, but it can be very fulfilling and encouraging. With a foundation of love and laughter—and typically a healthy amount of tears—like any other couple, whether it's two believers, two non-believers, or one of each in a relationship, we find creative ways of handling conflicts.

We once carried a cross together in a church, but now we might carry each other's materials for a service or class, carry a pack down a trail, or carry in the groceries.

Living life together with differing views on faith can be as good as it gets. It keeps the adventure of loving another person alive and creates daily opportunities to appreciate bridging barriers of belief for the best reason: You care for one another deeply, and the bridging is worth the effort.

We/They

An amusing cartoon pictures a man standing at the entrance to heaven reading a sign that says, "Welcome to Heaven: Keep Your Religion to Yourself." The angel next to him explains, "Ironically, that's what makes it so peaceful here."

The cartoonist hit the nail of truth on the head and raised an interesting question: What would happen if people kept their beliefs to themselves?

We all have a variety of beliefs about all kinds of things. Should we restrain ourselves from talking about anything we feel strongly about? I don't think so.

I think the point of the cartoon is simply that religious beliefs tend to stir the pot and can often hinder rather than create peaceful, harmonious relationships and conversations.

Many would say they feel "called" or even commanded to share their faith. They would be disobeying God if they kept their beliefs to themselves. I used to think this way. I remember passing around a booklet of "spiritual laws" that began by claiming, "God loves you and has a wonderful plan for your life." It seemed like a nice thing to say, except the next "law" stated that we are all sinners who deserve punishment for not loving the loving God. The subtext of the "wonderful plan" was, "Love me, or else."

Believers like me could never keep our faith to ourselves because we wouldn't be faithful.

Other believers may not show their religious feelings outside their place of worship. Their rituals, songs, sermons, and prayers are displayed within the walls of sanctuaries. When they exit their worship services, there isn't any meaningful way to tell what their beliefs are. They may wear a religious pin or necklace, or place a bumper sticker on their car, but generally their faith and beliefs are kept personal and private.

Some people of faith would say they don't need to talk about their beliefs because their life shows what they believe. Their faith is mostly non-verbal. They do good, compassionate work, and maybe they're motivated by faith, but they don't make a big deal of it.

An attention-grabbing crossover concerns those who wear religious clothing, not necessarily to flaunt their faith—it's just natural for them to wear it in public. We may think of a Catholic nun in the grocery store making a purchase from a Muslim cashier wearing a headscarf. Maybe we see two men on the street both wearing small caps. Is one a Jew and the other a Muslim? If so, what kind of Judaism, what branch of Islam?

Here's something to consider: What if we had to guess what someone believed? What would the world be like if we couldn't tell what religion someone subscribed to because no one advertised or talked about it?

Now that I'm a freethinking Humanist, this is something I like to test. I might be in a group of believers, reasonably and respectfully discussing some issue, and no one knows I'm not "one of them." Unless someone starts talking about the sacred or the supernatural, there is probably no way anyone would know a non-believing secular individual is in their midst.

I find this both comforting and instructive. When we put aside the "flags" we wave—the labels and identities we like to display—what's left? We're just people; people sharing the same communities and often the same concerns. We'd love to say we're a member of this or that group. There's nothing wrong with being proud of our affiliations. It's just that as soon as we start proudly self-identifying, the potential for division and misunderstanding arises. Instead of a collaborative environment, we may find ourselves in a W/T mode— We/They.

The history of religion reminds us of timeless, recurring messages—and these are not quiet or subtle messages. "DON'T keep your religion to yourself!" "Let your light shine for all to see." "The Word must be heard!" The message is loud and clear: Wherever you are, whatever you're doing, let everyone know you're a believer, one of

God's own. You must let them know what you have, and they don't have.

Aren't these sad and stressful messages? Why so much pressure to "proclaim the word" when there's so much more goodness to spread instead.

Not long ago, I spoke with an elderly clergyman who told me he knew Martin Luther King, Jr. They both served churches in the Atlanta area back in the 1950s. Some parishioners of this retired minister didn't want anything to do with Reverend King and didn't even want his children in their church school.

As I talked with this soft-spoken gentleman, he asked about my background. I gave him the thumbnail summary about leaving the ministry and becoming a freethinker. He seemed intrigued but didn't ask more questions. As he went his way, I wondered if my openness disturbed him.

Religious talk has a way of doing that sometimes, and without intending to, can help create a world divided by beliefs.

Frederick Douglass

When was the last time you heard a stirring speech that lifted you from your seat to cheer, cry, or both, as you witnessed the inspirational power of the human voice? I've heard very few with great rhetorical skill, who knew how to shape the art of public speaking to move the hearer. Now and then a voice will rise, and not always from expected corners of the community.

When I think of great speeches, my mind doesn't necessarily call up images from political platforms or preachers' pulpits, though some are memorable. I recall the evening an unhoused woman trembled before a packed sanctuary as she softly described how it felt to lose her family and home, finding herself living outside that very "sanctuary" in the cold and rainy holiday season. I think of a young painter and poet standing before a congregation to tell her story of living in a van behind a church while producing colorful art.

The voices that most resound and move us are rarely soothing or comforting—they can be alarming in their honest truth-telling.

The great abolitionist orator Frederick Douglass may not have left us his voice to ring in our ears, but his words still have a way of echoing in our collective conscience.

Born a slave in Maryland in 1818, he did not escape slavery until 1838 when he was twenty. As he stood to tell his horrific story before a Massachusetts anti-slavery meeting in 1841, few could have known that this young black man would become a great writer, publisher, and lecturer for human rights over the next fifty years, until his death in Washington, D.C., in 1895.

Friend of freethinkers and reformers like Elizabeth Cady Stanton, Douglass became a preacher of the "gospel of freedom," and not only for African Americans.

His *Narrative*, first published in 1845, the same year Henry Thoreau was sheltered in his Walden cabin, led to *My Bondage and My Freedom* in 1855, the same year Walt Whitman's *Leaves of Grass*, another radical book, appeared. The former slave's autobiography led to Frederick Law Olmsted to declare:

> What would Frederick Douglass have been had he failed to escape? What has he become since he dared commit the sacrilege of coming out of bondage? All the statesmanship.... has done less, in fifty years, to elevate and dignify the African race, than he in ten [years].[3]

In raising up his people and their cause, he was clear: "I feel that I have a right to speak and to speak strongly. Yet, my friends, I feel bound to speak truly."[4] Once bound in body, his mind was never restricted.

Douglass shook the foundations of both racial and religious institutions. One of his first speeches, in 1841, centered on "The Church and Prejudice," telling the story of his personal experience in Northern and Southern churches. In the South, his master would pray morning, noon, and night before whipping Frederick and his cousin while quoting passages from the Bible. As a freeman in the North, he experienced a different form of discrimination. For communion, "the white people gathered around the altar, the blacks clustered by the door." The white believers were served the bread and wine, then the minister called the black believers forward since, "you know God is no respecter of persons!" Douglass dryly concludes, "I haven't been there to see the sacraments taken since."[5]

In another church, Douglass saw a "great revival of religion" with many converts and baptisms. A little black girl was baptized "in the same water as the rest," but when she took communion, drinking from a common cup, a white girl sitting next to her stood and walked out of the sanctuary.[6]

For his "Reception Speech" at the Finsbury Chapel in England in 1846 his prophetic voice was sharp and resonant:

> But you will ask me, can these things be
> possible in a land professing christianity?
> Yes, they are so.... While America is printing
> tracts and bibles; sending missionaries abroad
> to convert the heathen...—the slave not only
> lies forgotten... but is trampled under foot by
> the very churches of the land. What have we
> in America? We have slavery made part of the
> religion of the land. [7]

Sounding like a prophet for our own times, he continued:

> I love that religion... which makes its
> followers do unto others as they themselves
> would be done by. If you demand liberty to
> yourself, it says, grant it to your neighbors. If
> you claim a right to think for yourself, it says,
> allow your neighbors the same right. [8]

Frederick Douglass left a well-polished mirror on the
podium or pulpit for us to see ourselves as we really are,
and to reconsider the ancient words, "the truth shall make
you free." He still challenges people of all colors with his
resounding voice of national conscience. He didn't merely
leave a mirror. He left a lens to read the old documents--
the Declaration of Independence and the Emancipation
Proclamation--more honestly and critically.

Douglass stands beside any leader today—on the steps of
congregation, courthouse or Congress—who is committed
to the hard work of emancipation far beyond political

speeches or sermons. Douglass stands tall, looks us in the eye, marches alongside, and speaks the truths we most need to hear and act upon. We walk with him, or we are left behind.

Native Drums

We're told that North Carolina has the largest number of Native Americans of any state east of the Mississippi—one estimate says there are 100,000. Of the eight recognized tribes here, the Eastern Band of Cherokee is the only one officially acknowledged as a sovereign nation by the federal government.

As Lakota holy man Black Elk said, there are many hoops —tribal circles with central fires—within the one big hoop of the Earth. Many of these hoops are still green and growing.

Robert appeared at our chaplaincy office in the San Francisco Bay area one afternoon. His long, dark hair and bronzed complexion gave away his native blood. He lived on the streets. From the Yurok Tribe in Northern California, Robert told me how he and his brother used to communicate with loud whistling across "the rez." You wouldn't want him to demonstrate that whistle in a closed space.

For an annual interfaith service, I asked Robert if he would carry an elk-hide drum made by a relative in Montana. Robert walked into the church beating the drum steady and slow. Along with several Native American friends, he chanted to "center us in the space." It felt like the history of Anglo-Native conflict was coming full circle there, with Native voices and drumming "creating sanctuary" in a local center of the white man's dominant religion.

Other Native women and men found their way into our welcome center. Talented guitarists, painters, and poets came through, and their presence was appreciated.

A few weeks following that service, Robert was found floating in the canal—a homicide victim. We led a memorial attended by many of his street friends as well as a pastor, priest, and rabbi who remembered his drumming chant. The same drum pulsated with our sad hearts as we remembered him that day.

I always will remember how Robert would call me "Crispy" in a loud greeting as he came in the door or met me on the street. A kind-hearted man with a good sense of humor, stories to tell, and a very loud whistle.

Born in Seattle, a city named for Chief Seattle (Si'ahl) of the Suquamish, and raised in a county named for the Snohomish, I never felt far from the "first peoples" of the Northwest. Through the years, as I visited the lands of the Skagit, Swinomish, Snoqualmie, Stillaguamish, Tulalip, Makah, Quileute, Quinault and other indigenous tribes, I had a disturbing awareness that my ancestors were complicit in the near-extermination of the original inhabitants of my own "native land."

We say "First Nations" for good reason. Washington State

has 29 recognized tribes, and we're told there may have been up to 500 "nations" across the continent before the United States was formed. These nations were nearly wiped out along with the buffalo, bear, and other original inhabitants, decimated by the obsessive scramble to "tame the frontier" and claim "God's country."

The word "savage" means untamed, uncivilized, wild. It comes from the Latin word "silvaticus" derived from "silva" or forest. A savage is a person of the forest, like a "pagan" is a person of the country and a "heathen" a person of the heath or heather. Anything savage can seem a threat to anything disconnected from wild Nature.

A savage person belongs to a "primitive" society. I've always thought that should be honored as "prime," "first," original—aboriginal. But we fear that wildness because our ways—including our religions—are not the ways of the wilderness.

Reading Vine Deloria and Dee Brown while in seminary, I was even more troubled by the tragic history, especially Brown's story of Wounded Knee. Deloria's theological work, *God is Red*, made much of the other theology I was reading seem weak and irrelevant.

Not long ago, I read *The Heart of Everything That Is*, a book that describes the compelling story of Sioux Chief Red Cloud and the resistance he led against the encroachment of gold-hunters and land-seekers in the 1860s. Red Cloud and his coalition of tribal groups were the protectors of over 700,000 square miles of land stretching from Canada to Kansas, from Montana to Minnesota. This territory "accounted for one-fifth of what would one day become the contiguous United States."

Political and military leaders were determined to force Red Cloud to give up the land for Western expansion. If their "treaties" didn't work, they would capture or kill him. He ended up leading "the only war [America] would ever lose to an Indian army." It's quite a tale.[9]

Looking back at the broken treaties and disastrous policies toward Native Nations, we would do well to keep in mind the worldview we have systematically attempted to silence: Everything is connected in a web of sacred relations.

Where does that drumming heart or whistle still sound?

Radical Presence

A brown thrush flew into the window one morning. Walking slowly to the glass, I saw it lying on the ground, beak open, panting. "You'll be ok. You're just stunned," I whispered. I left it alone, glancing out every few minutes until I saw it standing. A short time later, it flew.

That week, in the John Burroughs class I taught, we read selections from his first collection of nature essays, "Wake-Robin." He describes hearing the "evening hymn" of a thrush in a hemlock forest.[10] We discussed Burroughs' friendship with Walt Whitman and how he had suggested Whitman write a thrush into his great poem for Lincoln, "When Lilacs Last in the Dooryard Bloom'd."

The naturalist feels this "divine soprano" draws out "a serene religious beatitude" in him, a reverence in the stillness of the woods. He concludes by saying the feathered choir causes a "serene exaltation of sentiment of which music, literature, and religion are but faint types and symbols."[11]

Feeling that close to Nature, almost like walking into a deep green sanctuary, Burroughs senses something more meaningful than we can find in art or faith.

This all reminded me of a scene in John Steinbeck's, *The Grapes of Wrath* when the migrant father, Tom Joad, asks to talk with Casy, the preacher, sitting on the ground staring at his bare feet:

> Tom looked at Casy's waving toes. 'Could ya come down from your thinkin' an' listen a minute?' Casy turned his head on the stalk-like neck. 'Listen all the time. That's why I been thinkin'. Listen to people a-talkin', and purty soon I hear the way folks are feelin'. Goin' on all the time. I hear 'em and feel 'em; and they're beating their wings like a bird in an attic. Gonna bust their wings on a dusty winda tryin' ta get out ... [12]

In another scene, the tired and fading grandmother asks Casy to pray with her. Not so much for her but with her. He doesn't feel much like a preacher, so he says, "My prayers ain't no good ... I don't know what to say." The weary lady tells him, "Then say one to yourself. Don't use no words to it. That'd be alright." Casy has his doubts, so he replies, "I got no God." "You got a God," the grandmother says, "Don't make no difference if you don't know what he looks like." Reluctantly, the preacher bows his head in silence as the woman watches him. When he raises his head, she's relieved. "That's good; that's what I needed. Somebody close enough—to pray."

Preacher Casy doesn't understand what she means, but she goes on to voice one of the most profound lines in the book: "I'm just pain covered with skin." She knows that she's dying, and she wants to know another person is there with her—she's the bird beating its wings in the attic. [13]

With a wing and a prayer, we say.

Radical presence. Beyond words. Words mess it up. This calls up memories of the countless prayers of my chaplaincy years. In seven county jail facilities, I would lead prayers or meditations for inmate gatherings. We might be standing or squatting by steel bars, sitting quietly, or holding hands. It was about humans seeking something to bring meaning—a connected relation to other people. Some of the inmates were pain covered with skin. Some were feeling joy, others, sorrow, or fear. Whatever the reason for the request to pray, it seemed a silent presence was the best we could do, and it was good.

Interfaith prayer gatherings that included the "street community" were always deeply stirring. Chants by Native Americans and Buddhists. Scriptures from Muslims and Christians. Wisdom from Jews and Wiccans. Songs and stories from unhoused people.

We are told by some that a prayer must be offered "In the Name of [blank]." It seems that some who present themselves as masters of prayer think they have the special ear of God—invoking a divine name makes them appear to use the "king's seal" to assure He's listening.

I used to think there were "good prayers" and "bad

prayers." Now I think preacher Casy got it right, and so did old grandma Joad. Be with people, hear them, feel their pain, hear their wings beating against windows and doors, hoping to be free in the fresh air and sunlight. It doesn't matter what your God looks like, or even if you have a God.

Can we sit silently with someone and let them know we care enough just to be there? Or do we have to say something, speak to Someone else, to let them hear our words, our beliefs?

Maybe the best we can do sometimes is to whisper, "You're stunned. Hang in there. I'm here."

Secular Blessings

A hawk walked by today. You read that correctly. It walked. Chalk it up to yet another daily surprise from the mountains of Western North Carolina. It may have been the same small, white-breasted raptor we saw swoop down on a cardinal the day before. I thought at first the feathered feet crossing the yard belonged to a turkey or crow, but there it was: a hawk. It was walking—not hopping or flitting. I watched as it walked, then ran beneath the Rose of Sharon bushes and disappeared.

A hawk that walks. Something new to add to the natural procession passing by each day.

Some might say I'd been "blessed" to see this vision of nature's strange beauty. So many things are considered "blessings"—touches of the divine.

Millions say a blessing every day over meals. When I sneeze, my wife usually says, "Bless You," and she often thanks people with a smile and a "Bless You!" I believe she's sincere in this automatic gesture of graciousness.

But I have to say, blessings sometimes make me a bit uncomfortable.

There are blessings for everything, everyone, and every situation. In special ceremonies, animals are blessed, so are ships and buildings, babies and marriages. But what exactly *is* a blessing? What does it mean to bless and what would happen—bless me—if all these blessed blessings went unspoken?

In the years I was a Christian minister, I said many a blessing. You raise your hands or place them on a head or a shoulder. and you say something like "Bless You," "Blessings," or "God bless you." And you are expecting that those words actually *do* something. Even some of my pagan friends say "Blessed Be," and Buddhists bestow blessings on other beings.

But what do blessings really do? When I was a "blessor" I had to ask myself why I was blessing so much and so many. Did I need to bless the person, the food, the bread and the wine? Weren't they already good enough, blessed enough? Did I have the power—or the right—to make them "holy"?

In my decades as a chaplain I also gave blessings, but I knew I had no magic powers. I would say, "We all bless each other here and now," or something similar.

We know scriptures and traditions abound with blessings. In the Christian scriptures we read:

The *Lord* bless you and keep you.[14]

Blessed are you who are poor.[15]

May you be blessed.[16]

Blessed is the fruit of your womb.[17]

From the Qur'an: "The mercy of Allah and His blessings be upon you."[18]   Countless times we quote the ancient texts or speak the words, expecting something to happen, something to change.

Putting hands on another person and saying a particular word does not, in my experience at least, instantly bestow happiness or health or anything really. It may serve to make a person or congregation feel uplifted, and maybe that's ultimately the goal, to sense a caring touch.

If "blessing" originally had something to do with "making happiness happen," then who is qualified to give it or grant it?

It seems to me there is a sense that a blessing provides assurance—as the hymn says, "Blessed Assurance"—that people are making God very happy. So, it's really about *God's* happiness, not ours.

On the other hand, if a blessing asserts and affirms that the one who is doing the blessing speaks for the Creator of the Universe, and their touch is the *touch of God*— it seems more about the *blessor* than the *blessee*.

A blessing may be intended to assure a suffering person they are being "watched over," cared for, not only by "higher hands" but also by the "holy hands" of God's blessed representatives on earth.

When I was the blessor, it made me feel quite special, almost like I had special powers. It felt at times that I was passing something along—onto someone's head or bread. "As I touch you, God touches you; my words are God's words to you."

My clergy friends might respond: "It makes people feel God's presence when I touch their head or their bread, their house or their child. In a sacred manner, I am symbolizing God's good pleasure. I have no special powers."

Yet if a person "ordained by God" claims to bless others, offering consolation or confirmation of good favor from beyond, and if they truly share our full humanity, then couldn't we common folk equally offer a hand, hug, or an hour of our time in a similar way? Even giving a virtual embrace or an encouraging phone call in a time of physical distancing can share the goodness of human contact. And isn't that what we're actually looking for and truly needing? We can offer "secular blessings" regardless of religious beliefs.

Later in the morning, I heard a cry over the field. There was the "walking hawk" soaring across the valley. I was grateful to see it. I was touched by its beauty and felt naturally blessed. I was simply sensing the goodness and greatness of the wild world.

Poets often present us with a naturally undivided world, where blessings are literally rooted in nature and our nature. Mary Oliver writes:

> I don't know exactly what a prayer is.
>
> I do know how to pay attention,
>
> how to fall down
>
> into the grass, how to kneel down in the grass,
>
> how to be idle and blessed...[19]

Angels Aware

O ur friend burst into the youth group meeting with excitement. "I saw an angel at the door of the church!" he announced breathlessly. We ran out to see. No one was there, but his story sounded so believable. He told us a mysterious man was there, then vanished.

This happened during the period when our group was being split into the "church-going" believers and the "true" believers. There were the "ordinary" Christians and those of us who were "filled with the Spirit." A division had begun to form between some who had received the "full gospel" and those who were "only" born again.

Can you sense our youthful confusion?

Several of us had attended Pentecostal meetings where we were convinced that true power of the Holy Spirit was "moving in mighty ways" among us with great emotion and drama. We received the gift of "tongues" and spoke in "angelic languages." We had never felt the presence of God so deeply in our lives. It was so much more exciting than regular church!

When we brought this new "outpouring" back to the youth group, friends we'd known for years either joined the new movement or faded away. We felt badly, but we were confident that God had a special calling for us 16 and 17-year-olds.

Some of us started to see strange things. "Miracles" were happening all around us every day. One "sister" said she was saved in a car accident. Another claimed she had seen her deceased grandmother. A "brother" felt that God protected him from a fight at school. Another was certain God had helped him pass a test. I vividly remember lying in bed one night, pleading with the Lord to "show me a sign." I became terrified with the sense that a "heavenly presence" was in my darkened room. I hid under the covers and begged God to take the angel away.

Many folks don't know that in the Bible the word "angel" simply means "messenger." These are not the feathered fantasy creatures as depicted in old paintings or in Hollywood films. A man or woman "appears" with an important message. Three of these messengers came to Abraham in Genesis to eat, drink, and have a conversation.

Special messengers spoke to Joseph and Mary before Jesus' birth. Two men in dazzling clothes met the women at Jesus' tomb.

We absorb these images from an early age. It's not easy to "put aside childish things" in our imaginations.

In his excellent book, *The Better Angel: Walt Whitman in the Civil War*, Roy Morris, Jr. describes the poet's compassionate work among wounded soldiers. Whitman touched the lives of thousands, North and South, in the hospitals of Washington, D.C. during the war. As Morris states, "He had lived his ideals. If he was not literally an angel—and he never claimed he was—he was a more than passable substitute."[20]

"The better angels of our nature." We've all heard this phrase that Abraham Lincoln spoke at the close of his first inaugural address. But what does it mean? How are "angels" a part of our nature?

Lincoln was making a futile attempt to keep the southern states from seceding from the Union. His inaugural words are memorable both for their eloquence and for their failure. The "bonds of affection" he spoke of weren't strong enough to hold the Union together.

Whitman viewed the president as a kind of angel himself, though imperfect, down-to-earth, and quite mortal.

From time to time through my years in ministry, I would hear people refer to a nurse, social worker, or chaplain as an angel. I understood the sentiment but knew a person in crisis was simply thanking someone for being with them at the moment they most needed another person. It was a natural expression of gratitude for a very natural presence.

An oft-quoted verse from the thirteenth chapter of the book of Hebrews says that some believers had visits from messengers, but they didn't notice. They had "entertained angels unaware." [21]   Could that be because they were unaware that an ordinary person in their midst had something to teach? Or were they negligent in noticing their own "better angel" within?

This concept is suggested by the Hebrews passage. The community is instructed to love, to show hospitality to strangers, and to remember those in prison. This gives a twist to "love your neighbor." Your neighbor, even a stranger, may have a message for you—something you need to learn or be reminded of.

The stories of angels have been used for centuries to "prove" divine activity in the earthly realm. If people believe there are messengers sent to earth from above, that's their choice.

But why would we need them? Can those angels repair or build any bridges? We are the angels, the bearers of creative new thoughts, who bring extraordinary messages to ordinary circumstances where our better natures are called to rise and act.

Made for Cooperation

As I walked down the dimly lit hallway passing row after row of steel bars, I saw his black hands before I saw his face. "Donny" was gripping the cold bars of his cell while flexing his muscular arms over and over. He kept pushing and pulling even after greeting me with a "Hey, Chaplain!" and we began to talk about his day and the inter-faith service the previous Sunday. Like many of his fellow jail inmates, Donny attended the evening meetings out of curiosity and, as some admitted, to get out of the cell for an hour.

Donny and I stood there talking while the noise and activity of the jail flowed around us. He kept rocking back and forth, near the bars, then away. I stood close to hear him. I could see the sweat dripping from his shirtless chest. I thought, "A good-looking young man; so sad to think of the physical toll his drug use would eventually take on him and put him back inside again and again."

I'd been "visiting" Donny for several years. We saw each other passing on the street sometimes. Then, no surprise, I would see him behind the jailhouse bars once again.

That afternoon, while Donny was exercising to while away the hours, he had suddenly stopped. It wasn't always easy to tell if Donny was angry or just feeling intensely engaged with some thought. He pulled himself to the bars. Our faces were inches apart.

Staring at me intently, he put his head to the side and locked eyes with me. "You come in here week after week, year after year. You talk to us. You listen to us. You don't preach to us like some church people do." He flashed a knowing smile: "You show us what could be."

I asked him to explain that.

I don't remember Donny's explanation, but I remember the impression he left on me. As a young African American man who grew up in a mostly segregated neighborhood in a wealthy, liberal county, his life unfolded on the streets in the violent drug culture that instills a warped image of manhood.

What I heard Donny say was he saw me as a human being, a man of compassion—though my interfaith approach confused him a little. He was identifying a different model for what a person could do with their life, regardless of color or culture. I heard admiration, as well as a sense of loss. Most of all, I heard a spark of hopefulness, maybe even joy, when the shadow of the cell couldn't hide the momentary smile that crossed his face, the face of a different Donny. He saw me as I saw him: as a person, a man.

I met Donny in one of our weekly jail services on a Sunday evening. Men and women gathered separately, as members of diverse ethnicities and backgrounds, different faiths or no faith. And those jail services were memorable! The singing was wonderful. But the best part, at least for me, was the discussions.

Each week I would bring in a one-sheet handout with something to read and discuss. These papers often got passed around and discussed back in the cells. I still hold on to some of these, and one I recently found is a page of quotes from Marcus Aurelius, Roman emperor and philosopher born in the year 121.

We had some insightful conversation about the quotes I drew from his famous *Meditations*:

> People seek retreats for themselves, houses in the country, seashores, mountains; and you also desire these things very much. But everybody does that. Whenever you choose, you can retreat into yourself.[22]

No doubt, some women and men locked away and doing time found the concept of retreat encouraging.

> You are a runaway if you run from reason and good sense; you are blind if you shut the eyes of understanding; you are poor if you 'need' another, when you do not have—in yourself— all that is needed and useful in life.[23]

I'm sure we knocked that one around for a while.

"We are made for cooperation, like feet, like hands, like eyelids, like the rows of teeth. To act against one another, then is contrary to nature."[24] This was a particularly good reminder for people squeezed into small spaces for long periods of time.

"Do every act of your life as if it were the last, laying aside all carelessness and running away from what your head says is right..."[25] And this was a good invitation for inmates—and chaplains—to do some deep reflection.

"Within is the fountain of good, and it will always bubble up, if you will only dig."[26] Wise advice, imprisoned or not.

As our discussion ended, there was a sense that, like Donny, we all saw each other—with all our differences— as people, human beings, human bodies "made for cooperation."

What if the rest of us, not just locked up inmates, learned to see each other in this way, as diverse people, human beings, human bodies "made for cooperation." Could real community be far away or out of reach?

Tribal Nature

In her excellent book on National Parks, Terry Tempest Williams writes, "How do we find our way back to a world interrelated and interconnected, whose priority is to thrive and evolve?" Then she asks, "What kind of belief systems are emerging now that reinforce and contribute to a world increasingly disconnected from nature?"[27]

After visiting four different congregations over a period of a few weeks, I found myself musing on the interrelations and interconnections that we seem to be constantly searching for. Each of us searches for a community we can embrace, something we can hold on to.

Hearing faith leaders speak about "Our People" in what seemed a tribal sense got me thinking about the roots that ground and define us all. I quickly listed some categories that could describe my personal roots:

- Birthplace
- Family
- Hometown
- Home State

- Nationality
- Ethnicity
- Gender
- Language
- Politics
- Religion/Non-Religion

What would my filling in the blanks for each of these root categories tell someone about me? Would you "know" me if I told you these things? Maybe not, but at least you would have some "grounding," some context, for understanding who I am.

For each root, there is a story.

What happens when a group of people congregate to share their stories—comparing common tendrils of life from origin to personality to culture and more?

In a local synagogue, I sang and clapped while children wove through the sanctuary carrying tiny Torah scrolls. Each child carried the scriptures, the stories of their people, their culture, and their faith. There was something quite beautiful about the whole scene, especially as congregants touched each scroll or child in a kind of mutual blessing.

As a secular person, I also wonder how I could participate in that living ritual. On one level, I could. No one says I can't sing along and touch a Torah. On the other hand, it was beyond my reach—physically and figuratively. I could sing, clap and smile at the young faces, but I couldn't reach the aisle. If I could have, I'm not sure I would have chosen to "bless or be blessed" by the scrolls and their ancient story of one people who don't seem to be "my people," even though in some ways they are.

This, in a nutshell is both the upside and the downside of faith. The children are taught to hold tight to the traditions of their tribal ancestors while literally carrying forward the message—they walk in a pluralistic world where many tribes carry diverse stories, some more exclusive than others.

Terry Tempest Williams traveled to a number of National Parks, drawn to the beauty of the wild. She writes, "Nothing exists in isolation, especially not wilderness." A few lines later, she offers this thought: "Wilderness is not a place of isolation but contemplation."[28]

Some communities, particularly indigenous communities, accept the isolation of wild places since the land is home and, as Williams points out, "refuge." So, we set aside these wild places not to disconnect but to find some way to reconnect, to be refugees in a refuge in order to rediscover our need to contemplate, connect, and somehow communicate with Nature as our greater tribal community.

In a way, I'm trying to put into words something that may

be beyond words. Like Williams, we fill pages with sentences when the Big Story may never fit on a page, or in a book, or a library. We give it a shot, attempting to verbalize when verbs and nouns often blur and become unreadable.

Williams hands out phrases like walking sticks for the unexplored trails: "The call of the wild is not what you hear but what you follow." "Wilderness is the surprise of tenderness. The relationship we think is destroyed can be restored." "In wilderness, I see my authentic reflection in the eyes of Other."[29]

Reflection is required to comprehend her words. Maybe it makes more sense up the trail, out there, as we follow. And we have to ask, "Yes, but what or whom do we follow?"

Religion often steps onto the path and says, "Come this way; we will show the path; we will be your tribe." And perhaps we take that invitation for a day or a lifetime. We become trail-guides for others, handing out tightly bound maps for the next wanderers.

For others, like Williams—and like me—a love of wandering feels good and right. We are drawn to the mapless wilderness where children carry walking sticks of their own choosing, and we walk beside them or behind them, delighting in their wonder and that "authentic reflection" in their eyes. We also become aware of a myriad of eyes watching us, as an encircling tribe, out beyond a world that has forgotten.

Dismantling Fences

I'm a frequent visitor to the edges of faith and beyond. Exploring along the "border-lines" between any groups can be eye-opening and mind-opening. The fences are often well-defended but invite honest reaching out—and reaching across.

As I continue to reflect on the years when I imagined the world divided between "God's People" and everyone else, I often meet up with that wall in my head. It was very simple, or so we thought at the time: "God takes sides. We believe, so we are on God's side, and God is on ours." The dividing line was clear. Our chosen mission was to walk along this line and convince the world to cross over to our side. We were confidently on the road to the heavenly kingdom. All others were bound for hell.

To get more perspective on these "lines," I grabbed a local ginger beer and sat down with Jazz Cathcart, a founding pastor at Reach Life Church in Asheville. On any given Sunday, Jazz and co-pastor James Naisang lead 150 to 200 people in worship. Both of these youthful pastors wanted to form a *community* of believers with a focus on inner-city families. They seek "a village, not just an event" with a guiding sense that diversity means "things that bring us together are stronger than those that divide."

As Jazz sees it, "ethnic, socio-economic and generational diversity," are addressed by the "core message of the gospel." In this view, the emphasis is on breaking barriers to emphasize "one race"—the human race—rather than trying to be "interracial."

Jazz consults with other congregations on how to foster diversity, and he has relationships that include members of the Muslim, Jewish, and secular communities/mindsets. Those with no faith affiliation visit his church, and some choose to become believing members.

His love for the Reach Life "family," a word he uses frequently, is evident. Another image he likes to use is that this family is growing like an oak tree. It's "healthy, patient growth," he says.

Outside the church, he feels it's essential to be "sensitive, gentle, and aware toward others loved by God." It's critical for a believer to "share the message with your life, not just your lips."

These topics always jar my curiosity into an awakened state, and this conversation was no different. So, I asked how he and his congregation viewed people of other faiths and non-believers like me. Jazz looked me straight in the eye: "I do believe you're going to hell." He smiled as he pronounced judgment on me, but everything else—his body language and tone of voice— emphasized how sincerely he believed what he was saying. Raising my eyebrows, I thanked him for his honest, unequivocal statement—at least I knew where I stood, and my feet were getting hot.

I stood my ground as we launched into a discussion of some of the classic arguments for and against a place of divine punishment. I used the word "torture," but Jazz softened it, so to speak, to "torment." "Given that so many good people who have lived well are sent to hell," I said. "I 'd rather go where they are."

Jazz held firm and continued to articulate his defense of the faith—what theologians call apologetics—with an abundance of confidence. I reminded him that I once saw the world as he does. I remembered an earlier comment Jazz made that he rarely finds "an open-minded liberal willing to change their mind." I wondered: How open is a committed believer to changing their mind?

I had changed my mind—radically! That change only happened to me through years of honest reflection.

I was particularly impressed hearing Jazz describe his work outside the walls of the church. He goes into jails to speak with prisoners and joins members of his church in serving breakfast one Saturday each month on downtown streets. He's particularly proud of the Urban Mentoring Academy he founded and directs. In his words, the academy is "a non-faith-based, secular organization" pairing mentors with high school students in Asheville.

As I half-joked with Jazz, "Maybe this is where the heaven-bound and hell-bound are finding some common ground." We got up to leave, sharing a tight handshake and a hug.

As I walked up the street back to my car, I reflected on my conversation with Jazz. Until we humanize each other beyond the fences and borderlines, the colors and creeds, we're doing little more than guarding the walls.

We have to ask ourselves if we truly want to spend our lives "holding the line" along the guarded boundaries or make an effort to learn about those on the other side. Instead of taking sides, might we begin to dismantle the fences standing side by side?

I'm grateful that Jazz was so willing to discuss his views and to consider new ways of reaching out toward a shared, common life. He may think I'm heading toward simmering torment in eternity, but somehow, I think we found cooler ground that day.

Open Tables

Back in my jail chaplaincy days, I led seven interfaith services each week. These were very informal, of course, since they were held in guarded dining halls, locked cells, through steel bars, in courtyard cages made of bladed wire, or in concrete hallways. Yet, now and then, I would put on my Christian minister "hat" and let inmates know that our gathering that day would have a decidedly Christian flavor. Sometimes this meant we would be discussing a Bible passage or theme. At other times, I would invite anyone who wanted to join us to "celebrate communion" (The Eucharist, Lord's Supper, Last Supper, Breaking Bread). I made it very clear that everyone was welcome. No one was required to be a Christian to share "The Meal."

One evening I brought in some crackers and white grape juice. A woman in a yellow jumpsuit joked that maybe God would turn the juice to wine. A man in a green jumpsuit wondered why I didn't bring a loaf of warm fresh bread. I wish I could have. Jail staff were strict about what could and could not be brought inside. We made the best of it.

On this night, Bob, a young Jewish man, asked if he could join. "Good to have you," I responded. We all had a very lively discussion about the meaning of the "sacrament," sang a few folk songs, and shared a brief prayer. I gave each prisoner a cracker and poured juice into little cups to drink. "This is God's Body," I would say, or, "You are a part of God," or something similar. The point was that no one was left out and everyone was included—no matter what. Who was I to tell someone they couldn't celebrate Life, have a taste of "grace," or feel a part of the "community of faith" or any community at all?

We finished the celebration and stood around chatting. While a young tattooed guy strummed my guitar, Bob asked if he could drink the last of the grape juice I had poured in the wooden chalice. I handed it to him. He told me they never had a drink in the mess hall that tasted that good.

Afterward, as I carried my guitar and the empty box of crackers out into the night air, I smiled and shook my head thinking of how many in the Christian world would be aghast at what I'd done. Surely there have to be rules for those who partake! This "sacramental" experience is only for "God's People," right? We can't allow just anyone, can we?

Then, an ironic image struck me—a Jewish person at The Last Supper!

Have you ever been excluded from Communion? I have. My wife has. Some churches are very strict about who can "partake" of the "elements"—bread and wine.   The language used by the officiant can be clear: "Don't touch this if you're not a believer like us!" I once saw an elderly woman turned away by a priest when she came forward for the elements. I never returned there, and I doubt she did either.

You might be asking yourself why a nonbeliever, a person who doesn't believe that Jesus was more than a human being, would even want to share the Supper. It seems to me we ought to consider the deeper meaning of a final meal among friends and whether Jesus of Nazareth intended it to be anything more than a dinner shared "in remembrance of Me." I don't have to accept everything he said as true for me, but I can honor and respect his life given in service of others, especially those who are poor, treated unfairly, or excluded (irony alert).

At times, I've sat with family members in a service and chosen to take a piece of bread. Other times I choose not to—though that can be pretty awkward to be the only one.

During seminary, I attended a Catholic mass every Sunday. Oddly enough, it was part of my job. As an instructor at a private school with developmentally disabled students, I would walk down with them to the "Gym Mass" held in a Catholic school. These remarkably hospitable services were led by young priests. Learning that I was a seminary student, a priest would sometimes invite me to hold the chalice or bread during The Eucharist. I felt honored and respected. A few of my students sometimes held the chalice and bread—a radical gesture of welcoming.

Communion never meant more than when I shared it with those who felt the most excluded. When I felt welcomed, it was natural to welcome others. If a person feels that this inclusiveness offends Jesus, I wonder: how can we turn anyone away from a table when the host is Love?

In a world divided by beliefs, we need more open tables. Building on radical inclusiveness might look strange and chaotic at times, but when the table gets larger, the feast somehow tastes better.

Higher Ethics

My first year in seminary, the Dalai Lama of Tibet came to campus to open a new library of Buddhist literature. This caused quite a stir since he's a head of state, a world figure, and of course a Buddhist. He was welcomed graciously, and many of us got to see and hear him up close. In our yearbook, my roommate Tom, a professional photographer, secretly slipped in a photo of this great man of peace under the name, "Ocean of Wisdom." Some of us would have enjoyed having him remain as a professor. It was fun to imagine him sitting with us in class or sneaking up to play ping pong in the bell-tower. We would have loved to knock around our theologies with him.

As a refugee from his homeland of Tibet for more than 60 years, he calls himself "India's longest-staying guest."[30] Millions of followers make pilgrimage to "be in his presence" and the 85-year-old travels the globe with his message of lovingkindness and compassion, all the more meaningful coming from someone never allowed to return to his homeland.

It would be remarkable if a world faith leader published a book entitled, *Beyond Religion*, but that's just what the Dalai Lama did in 2011. Finding and reviewing my copy,

I was impressed and inspired once again by one of the great voices of reason in our world today.

In the opening pages of his book, he remarked that prayerful meditation is vital to him, and he was grateful to know people had been praying for him during a hospital stay, but he admitted it was more comforting to know the doctors and hospital staff were well equipped to respond to his illness.

The first line in his first chapter, "Rethinking Secularism," presents his wonderful perspective: "I am a man of religion, but religion alone cannot answer all our problems."[31] His reasonable honesty is a welcome refreshment.

Then he presents the heart of the book:

> What we need today is an approach to ethics which makes no recourse to religion and can be equally acceptable to those with faith and those without: a secular ethics.[32]

> I am of the firm opinion that we have within our grasp a way, and a means, to ground inner values without contradicting any religion and yet, crucially, without depending on religion.[33]

He uses a very natural and common analogy to describe what he means by "secular ethics." Ethics without religion

are like water. Ethics with religion are like tea—flavoring
has been added. But, he says, "While we can live without
tea, we cannot live without water."[34] That's a powerful
analogy, something to sip and savor.

On the central practice of compassion, he writes:

> Those with religious faith have rich resources
> for the cultivation of compassion, and
> religious approaches can also be great
> resources for humanity as a whole. But
> religion is not necessary for cultivating
> compassion. In fact, secular techniques for
> compassion training are already in use, and
> their effectiveness has even been scientifically
> demonstrated.[35]

Regarding attachment to one religion or another, he offers
this guidance: "[As] a Buddhist, I should strive not to
develop excessive attachment toward Buddhism. For to do
so would hinder my ability to see the value of other faith
traditions."[36]   This wise Tibetan monk offers a curative
model for our culture's OCD-like religious attachments.

Much of what "His Holiness" teaches may seem too
idealistic. He responds:

> To some, this idea of universal compassion
> may sound too idealistic and possibly even
> religious. As for its being too idealistic, I don't
> think it is. Many things that we now take for

granted, such as the notion of universal education, would have sounded too idealistic in the past, but now are thought of as entirely practical and indeed necessary. As for the suggestion that the idea of universal compassion is religious, I disagree. Certainly, some people's selflessness and service to others are rooted in their religious devotion, such as serving God. But at the same time, there are countless others in the world today who are concerned for all humanity, and yet who do not have religion.[37]

I've seen the Dalai Lama in person several other times through the years—once at an international youth conference and another time with Archbishop Desmond Tutu. He always makes you think—and laugh. His contagious sense of humor invites listeners to see him as a human being while seriously considering the truth of his teachings.

One gift of Buddhism is that while you are gently nudged to calm your mind and be mindful, the teachings always make you think more! Quiet your head but use it.

We can't all be an "ocean" of wisdom. But perhaps all we need is a cupful, a handful, or even a drop.

Risky Trust

S tanding close to the dusty steel bars, near the end of a dimly lit corridor, I was speaking quietly with "Andre," a young African American man awaiting trial for a drug charge. This was the typical setting for a chaplain visit—a rather bizarre venue for hearing, let alone meaningful listening to a person in crisis.

The television, bolted to the wall, blended its blaring nonsense with all the other televisions down the line. Add to this din the voices of a hundred other men, doors slamming, and people shouting through the facility, and you get a sense of the senselessness of having a quiet, let alone private, conversation. And it was all in stark contrast to the outside world of nature that I love so much.

As I heard Andre tell me the pain he felt for the way his actions hurt his grandmother, his sense of loss, and his struggles with addiction that kept bringing him back behind bars, suddenly, the steel door opened automatically, and we were standing face to face.

"Gonzales! Roll it up!" yelled the sheriff's deputy from the other end of the corridor. I stepped aside as an older Latino man rolled up his mattress from the floor and wrestled it out the door, stumbling down the line to the awaiting deputy. Gonzales was being released. The other men in the cell quickly stretched out, glad to have a little more breathing room in the overcrowded space—at least until the next booking.

The heavy cell door closed with a thud. Andre and I picked up our conversation.

This snapshot offers a small glimpse into a practice of chaplaincy for which neither church, seminary, nor faith adequately prepared me.

I was often aware and amazed how trusted I was throughout the jail. Left to wander unmonitored, locked in with the hundreds of men and women in their separate units, I felt invisible at times, attempting to care for the locked-up inmates as best I could moving about "under the radar" of jail security. (Ironically, the word "security" comes from a Latin word meaning "without care.")

Jail commanders made all the difference, as did desk sergeants. If they were by-the-book people with a heavy-handed approach to managing the facility, I might be restricted in my movements and not as respected for my role. If it was clear they were more easy-going and seemed to actually care about prisoners, I might even be consulted from time to time. This was true with one lieutenant who walked with me through the units, smiling at inmates, shaking hands, and asking people how they were. We talked about the noise level. He was aware that the clatter made it harder for both inmates and staff. He spoke with me about ways to make the steel doors close without constantly slamming (in the "slammer").

On my rounds each week I asked to be locked into the Protective Custody (PC) cell where eight to ten men were separated from the rest of the jail due to the serious nature of their charges.   These were men accused of rape, molestation, domestic violence and even murder.   There were older and younger men in the PC cell with an array of backgrounds, ethnicities, and sexual orientations. Some were there simply because the administration didn't know where else to keep them safe from those who might wish to harm them.

The most segregated offenders were offensive to the rest of the jail population, including some staff. People would often ask me why I would go in to see "those guys."

Protective Custody was a strange place with a strangely calming atmosphere at times—a good setting for a chaplain to be "real."   Mostly there were "private" conversations with men while they were sitting on their bunks. If a group of the guys wanted a "service," the television would be switched off, and we would sit at the steel table surrounded by others sitting and lying on their bunks. We would sing a few songs, listen to a reading—a poem, scripture, or wise thought—and engage in some deep discussion or light banter with laughter. Then we'd share a quiet, prayerful meditation and sing a closing song. Several men were very talented musicians who would strum my guitar or add an inspiring voice to our singing.

In these moments, we were all humanized, in some sense, separated from the offended world.

Sounds a bit crazy, doesn't it—to have such meaningful, even delightful, moments and hours locked in with people accused of such terrible things.

And it was important to remember they were "accused," not convicted. Jail is not prison. Though some are sentenced to jail-time, most people in jail are waiting—"detained"—before or during trial since many cannot afford bail. Or, they may simply be waiting to be released—in a few days, weeks, or months. If someone is found guilty, they may be moved to a prison.

For a chaplain, just being inside, present with people, guilty or innocent, becomes a privilege that is hard to describe.

It takes an open mind, an open heart, open eyes, and listening ears to make a difference in the closed places securely hidden from the rest of us in the "free world." But it's not just in these hidden places where an open, listening attitude is required.

It doesn't really matter where you are, building community requires trust. Building trust takes time, involves risk, and requires healthy boundaries. But if more of us could learn to trust more, we might find some new freedom piercing the steel bars in our heads.

Extinguish Evil

We hear it all the time, and probably think it too: "That's *evil*" or "They're *evil*." Add a "D" and, no surprise, we have "Devil."

As the dictionary puts it, evil describes something "profoundly immoral and malevolent; (of a force or spirit) embodying or associated with the forces of the devil; harmful or tending to harm."[38]

Evil is "wickedness, and depravity, especially when regarded as a supernatural force."[39] Someone gives you the *evil eye* or you have *evil thoughts*.

In the Bible, we read of *The Evil One*, and we know exactly who that is: Satan, the adversary of God—created by God—and up to no good. In the first book of Peter, this nasty creature is lurking around: "Like a roaring lion your adversary the devil prowls around, looking for someone to devour."[40] This metaphor plays on our fears of wild animals and of the wilderness itself. Stay inside the locked doors (of the faith) because there be dragons beyond.

The solution? According to the book of James in the Christian scriptures: "Resist the devil, and he will flee from you."[41] Stand your ground face to face with a hungry lion, and he'll run away. That would be something to see!

A homeless veteran I knew had a unique perspective. He liked to say, "*Evil* spelled backward is *live*." When we live our lives with goodness, we keep evil away. Simple yet profound.

The concept of evil with a dark powerful force behind it saturates our contemporary culture, especially in our films. "The Dark Side" versus "The Force" is played out in hundreds of ways. In the shadows lurks the bad stuff, the bad guy, the terrors and horrors that haunt our dreams and heighten our fears.

Some people exploit these fearful images and feelings. They speak of *evil empires*, *evil nations*, and *evil leaders* of *evil countries* out to do *evil things* to us. The worst case is when individuals are called *evil*, and they become less than human—*monsters*.

Strangely, hearing about all these evil entities makes us feel better because we're not evil monsters, are we? Surely not. We could never do "those evil things," right?

Another instruction from the book of James is, "Do not speak evil against one another."[42] Does this biblical writer understand that calling others "evil," even when they do "evil things," can be "evil" in itself?

This is where it gets weird. The origin of our word "weird" is "wyrd," an Anglo-Saxon word suggesting something supernatural or uncanny, something controlling destiny or fate.[43] Some would consider "the weird" as evil. When something or someone is just "too weird," we reach for the most convenient word: *evil*.

And our tendency to call things or people "evil" when something happens that's just too terrible for words, reveals our own shadow, our own fears, our own inner lions. At least it seems so.

Partly for this reason, I would suggest it's time we eliminate the word *evil*. Apart from our mythologies and famous legends, the term is unhelpful at best, and harmful—*evil*—at worst. That's the circle: *Evil is evil*. Using the word can be "harmful or tending to harm."

During my ten years as a jail chaplain, I was often locked in—quite literally—with people the community labeled as *monsters* or *evil sub-humans*. One woman was accused of stabbing another woman to death; another, of killing her child; another, of assaulting a young girl. One shot a local clergyman. These were dreadful crimes—all deserving of severe punishment.

Yet, as I learned—pushing through my own personal fears and revulsion over their brutal actions—they were each human beings. I knew them by name, talked with them, prayed with them, and hugged them. These were individuals who were charged with some truly horrible things.

Horrible: to cause trembling or shudder—and I did. Yet I had to acknowledge that they were human beings who were alive like me. We shared the same breath of life within those prison walls—even though some of them had taken that life from another person. This awareness put "being human" into perspective, and it wasn't a comfortable experience.

We can either choose to view the world as *good* and *evil*, *God* and *Devil*, or we can choose to see the world as ours, with all kinds of people, some who do some extremely bad things that deserve clear-headed, lion-hearted responses at a societal and individual level.

When we separate something or someone from us and slap on the label *evil*, we suspend our reason, our ethics, and our conscious ability to cope with something bad. It's too easy to turn evil into **Evil** and personify our fears to make us feel better. Could it be **D-Evil** is our big, scary shadow cast on the walls of our minds?

To face our humanity honestly, to see ourselves as we really are, facing our own weaknesses is the opposite of "evil."

Broken people and broken minds, like broken bridges, may still be salvageable. We should never throw anyone away, or hide them away, thinking that will magically make us a better, less *evil* community.

As humans we can find places of meeting, even in the

rubble of fallen bridges: jails, prisons, treatment centers, and halfway houses. And on occasion we may find ways to offer an outstretched hand to help one person climb out of the wreckage.

Faith in Questions

In a conversation over Zoom, my friend Charles, an Episcopal priest, asked why I don't define "faith" in my writings. He said I do a good job explaining "secular" and "freethinking," but he wanted to hear what I have to say about "faith."

I write so much about faith, but I suppose I don't think to attempt to nail it down because I'm slightly skeptical of definitions in these matters.

My priest friend offered me an alternate use of the word. He said, "I have faith you are a good person." That was a use of the word I could accept without pondering. We agreed to continue the conversation sometime soon.

Later, as I was reflecting on what he said, I came up with some other responses to his comment: "So, you take it by faith that I'm a good person?" Or, "You see my life, come to know me, and then make an informed decision, coming to the conclusion that I'm a decent guy?" I suspect that's not what most people mean when they use the word faith.

Charles continued our dialog via email. I smiled at his first statement: "I believe faith at its heart has much less to do with a particular set of beliefs, than with a foundational trust that something is reliable."

He grew up thinking that faith and belief were attached to a particular religion. His thinking changed over the years as his questions increased, and the church didn't seem to welcome his questions. He felt that he lost his faith, and for a period preceding his call and ordination, stopped attending church.

He said, "After I left the church, and to this day, the natural world and art, especially poetry, filled the yearning space within me." He felt a "reassuring sense" that he was part of something much bigger than himself. This enticed him "to grow toward ... goodness and active love."

He eventually returned to church, partly due to a desire for his family to experience "the deepest values that guided my life." He went on to ordination when he realized his "questions could be an asset for ministry."

His next line was stunning and refreshing: "I've had faith in questions ever since."

Charles became the founding Executive Director of the United Religions Initiative, a remarkable international, interfaith organization formed in 2000. While building relationships across borders with all kinds of people around the world, he discovered that "at our heart we shared a faith in the fundamental goodness of human beings, a faith that the power of love was ultimately sovereign and a faith that if we connected with each other and acted in the world [representing goodness and love] the world would be a more peaceful and just place."

Though I usually don't use the word faith in the same way Charles does, I'm right with him on the way to "live faithfully" in the sense he describes.

There are several ways to describe faith.

Faith can be defined as "complete trust or confidence in someone or something," or "strong belief in God or the doctrines of a religion, based on spiritual apprehension rather than proof." It can also refer to "a system of religious belief," or "a strongly held belief or theory."[44]

Many people "have faith." Others say they are "people of faith." Some are members of a particular religious "faith." Others argue that faith is not belief, but faith and belief are closely related. A faithful individual has a set of beliefs but might say they "trust in God," which is how they practice their faith within a certain "faith tradition."

Some say nonbelievers actually "have faith" in science or reason or the fact that the sun will rise in the morning. I don't see it that way. To me, these expectations are not faith but instead are reasonable conclusions drawn from experiential evidence. The fact the sun will rise in the morning isn't about faith. In fact, our investigative reasoning tells us the sun doesn't "rise" at all. Which, in itself, presents a good example of how faith differs from fact.

I'm confident or I could say I *trust* that Charles, and others like him in religious communities who understand faith in this way, can be open to walking and working side by side with freethinkers and nonbelievers.

When the emphasis is on relationships that are built upon trust, then creeds, theologies, churches, religions, and believing itself can become less important than the people who are working together to build new bridges and form new connections.

In Charles' words, "faith has long ceased to be about believing [in beliefs] … faith is a deep and abiding trust in what I have perceived to be the sovereign power of love and goodness."

Does this leave serious questions about faith in our world? Of course. But now, as believers or nonbelievers, we have a choice. We can choose to trust one another, and we can trust our questions about faith and life to be assets on the way forward.

Repairing Brokenness

As a chaplain in jails and on the streets, I moved among countless men and women whose addictions ruled or ruined their lives. Often, these addictions were direct causes of the unwise decisions that landed a person behind bars or behind bushes without a home.

I mostly counseled and conversed with people struggling with drugs or alcohol, but there are many forms of addictions. Many seek the rush, the thrill of some altered state of consciousness and "higher" feeling—an escape. Yet, as most of us find out in life, the "highs" can lead right down to the "lows." What goes up, must come down.

Someone gets high, and they hurt another person, or they hurt themselves. The human toll is immense, costing lives and resources that should wake us up to a troubling fact: We live in an addicted culture from alcohol to opioids to device screens. And this isn't just a poor person's problem. Addiction to profit, power, self-image, shopping, and much more—in our endless accumulation of stuff and things—makes us sick.

Pat was an alcoholic. Joe was a druggie. Jen was both. Each was a smart, gentle person—until they used. They would help others or volunteer to clean our drop-in center. But they couldn't stay "clean" and were judged "unclean" so they were locked up, out of sight, in a dirty cell. They may have been "SOS"—Stuck on Stupid—but they weren't stupid; they were trapped and needed a way out.

Unless people get help while they're locked up, chances are they'll be back out using. "Using." There's a word to think about long and hard. What's being used, and who's being used? The revolving doors of the jails, shelters, and treatment centers spin round and round, just like the lives that are caught, trapped, and used.

We know that addiction is a disease. We see how it affects everyone. Thankfully there are ways to end the destruction and begin the healing. When people finally decide they are killing themselves and harming others—they may be ready to admit they're helpless. It's called "hitting bottom."

Alcoholics Anonymous and Narcotics Anonymous have been around a long time and work for many people. I have friends who are in recovery, and I know "the program" keeps them going—sometimes keeping them alive. I brought the *AA Big Book* or *Each Day a New Beginning* devotional into the jail when someone requested a copy.

It may not be common knowledge that there are alternatives to these faith-centered recovery programs. These are good programs and treatments without "higher powers" and religion-based support. AA and NA say a person does not have to be a person of faith to work the program, but it is about "God as we understand God." And many of the twelve steps direct a person to God in some form. This is fine for many people. But the language is excluding for those who are nonbelievers.

Secular AA, SMART (Self-Management and Recovery Training), SOS (Secular Organizations for Sobriety), and Rational Recovery are among the options available to secular persons who struggle with addiction.

One lively discussion I led in jails focused on Father Leo Booth's book, *When God Becomes a Drug: Breaking the Chains of Religious Addiction and Abuse.* Booth, an Episcopal priest, understands that "religious addiction, like alcohol addiction, is a dysfunction that can be treated."[45] It was enlightening to discuss this among inmates of diverse races, beliefs, and economic levels. Most had never considered the idea that religious faith could be another addiction that needed "recovery."

Religious addiction is often unrecognized but can lie beneath and can even generate other addictions.

Consider guilt. If a person is told for years they are a "sinner"—forgiven but constantly having to ask forgiveness—they may feel they can never be good enough to please an unhappy, strict Father in the sky. This can lead them to turn toward destructive behavior.

Or look at belief itself. A person may have doubts or feel they no longer believe the "right" things. On top of the guilt, there is fear of punishment. The lower in hell someone feels, the "higher a heavenly high" they crave. It's hard to break free from that cycle.

There's another aspect to religious addiction that may be overlooked: repeating the same words or behaviors over and over without thinking. The mind is unplugged or on pause, while praying, singing, reciting, or going to a service. If these behaviors become compulsive—"I *have* to do this!"—addictive behavior emerges.

If we can recover our reasonable selves and take the honest steps—2, 12, or 20 steps—toward health, we can choose responsible freedom, and we can reconnect with family, friends, and community.

That sounds like sobriety, sanity, and good sense.

Better than Unity

While serving as a chaplain with the "unhoused community," we organized the first interfaith prayer service in our county north of San Francisco. We welcomed the homeless community, which made sense since the prayer service was held in the Saint Vincent de Paul free dining room, a hub for houseless folks.

As we were lining up speakers and musicians, I called a local church pastor to ask if he would like to join us and offer a prayer. He told me he would need to talk with his staff and get back to me. A few days later, he called to say, "We prayed about it and decided we could not in good conscience pray with people of other faiths." I was disappointed but thanked him for considering and hung up the phone. I shook my head and let it go.

The evening of the gathering, we had a good crowd attending. There were representatives from many traditions and a nice mix of neighbors with and without homes. We heard from a Catholic priest, a Jewish rabbi, several Protestant ministers, and others.

Highlights included chants by a Native American elder and a Buddhist priest as well as songs led by members of the street community. It was one of the most memorable services during my ten years as a chaplain and served as a model for other inter-religious gatherings over the years.

I often wonder why we don't hear about more of these kinds of gatherings that are welcoming to all folks. It seems so natural and healthy for a community to hold events that openly invite and include a diversity of people and viewpoints. In my opinion, this is the only way forward—if we genuinely want to move forward.

Years later in Asheville, through my wife Carol, I learned that a group was meeting nearby to plan a spring conference at Lake Junaluska near Waynesville, North Carolina.

I asked George Thompson, a retired Methodist minister and Chair of the Executive Committee that was planning the meeting, if he would describe the intent of the conference. He said the conference was "designed to attract people of all faiths or no faith that have a heart for building peace in their communities."

Thompson said the meeting would be hosted by the Lake Junaluska Assembly as a regional program of the United Methodist Church, and added, "The committees that plan and execute the event are composed of persons from various Protestant denominations and the three Abrahamic faiths (Jewish, Islamic, and Christian)."

George told me that the conference theme was "Meeting the Other: Can We Talk?" He saw the theme as an invitation to "all participants to reach out to those that are different from one's self, bridging divisions of misunderstanding, racial [tension], gender bias, and generational divide."

Keynote speakers included Rabbi Nancy Fuchs Kreimer, a leader with extensive multi-faith experience, the Rev. T. Anthony Spearman, pastor of an African Methodist Episcopal Zion Church in Greensboro and current president of the North Carolina NAACP, and Professor Juliane Hammer, an Islamic Studies scholar at the University of North Carolina, Chapel Hill.

Rabbi Kreimer's profile caught my attention when I read that she was leading a campus chaplaincy project in Pennsylvania that includes chaplains from five major faiths as well as Humanists.

The Lake Junaluska meeting included a dialogue session with the three keynote speakers "to involve the participation of more diversity of age, ethnicity, faith, and gender." And there was an evening performance by "Abraham Jam," a Muslim, Jewish, and Christian trio whose website states, "harmony, where we sing different notes that are beautiful together, is even better than unity, where we all sing the same note."

One aim of the gathering was to "model with civility and respect how to communicate within a culture of contentious diversity while upholding our various core values and religious traditions."

Tammy McDowell, Assistant Director of Programming at Lake Junaluska, commented: "In these polarizing times, it is exciting and hopeful to see a diverse group of people gathering together to discuss their differences with love and respect."

Rabbi Phil Bentley, also on the committee, told me the goal was "to help people learn how and why to reach out to people who we might consider 'other.'" He said that early youthful experiences between Jews and Christians led him to be "involved in inter-faith activities and councils everywhere I lived and worked throughout my life."

The 2018 "Meeting the other: Can we talk?" event achieved its goals with flying colors, and all of its stated objectives seem even more relevant today.

We need more conferences like this one in more communities, meetings that seek to move all types of people forward along a progression in religion that I call the "Three C's": from *Competitive* to *Comparative* to *Cooperative*.

3 C's

One of the great modern scholars, mystics, and social activists, Rabbi Abraham Joshua Heschel, wrote about how religion can become sinful.

Religion becomes sinful when it begins to advocate the segregation of God, to forget that the true sanctuary has no walls. Religion has always suffered from the tendency to become an end in itself, to seclude the holy, to become parochial, self-indulgent, self-seeking; as if the task were not to ennoble human nature but to enhance the power and beauty of its institutions or to enlarge the body of doctrines. It has often done more to canonize prejudices than to wrestle for truth; to petrify the sacred than to sanctify the secular.[46]

If the rebel rabbi was correct, then what are we to think, what are we to do, about contemporary religion? Has religion itself become "sinful"? Does a faith that espouses a separation of the divine and human, sacred and secular, miss the mark—the classic definition of sin—when it sets itself apart as the sole container for the Creator?

Hold those questions.

When facilitating classes and discussion circles I sometimes draw attention to the "Three C's" as they relate to religion: *Competitive, Comparative, Cooperative.*

Competitive religion may be the most familiar. It's relatively simple. People think, say, or imply: "Our beliefs and our God are better. We win!" No one usually says that, but we know competitive faith when we see or hear it. "God is on our side" or "We are God's favorites" are examples of this attitude. There are clear winners and losers, insiders and outsiders, saved and unsaved. "Heaven is for us. Hell is for you." This reminds me of the dodge-ball games we played as kids, or any competitive sports. Someone comes out on top. Others are eliminated.

Comparative Religion was my favorite subject to study and to teach for a long time. I still appreciate an academic approach that focuses on comparing belief systems. It can be quite thought-provoking to place faith traditions, their histories, scriptures, creeds, and worldviews side by side for comparison.

My feeling is that courses in Comparative Religion could and should be taught, not only in congregations of all faiths but in secular settings including public schools. A tricky prospect, I agree, but worthwhile if instructors are well-trained. But there's the rub. Who is prepared to teach Religion from a balanced, cultural perspective? If qualified teachers can't be found to provide a non-sectarian approach to Comparative Religion or the Bible as literature, I don't see how these can be competently taught.

Obviously the second "C"—*Comparative*—only works in non-fear-based settings. When a group is fearful of being challenged by new ideas and beliefs (the god-segregators), comparative study and open discussion is unwelcome. In other words, those whose faith has already "won," are probably not going to engage in any serious comparisons with the "losers."

Without some knowledge of other traditions, we have no foundation for appreciation or actual dialogue. If wisdom is the goal, more extensive reading and experience is necessary, beginning with encounters in diverse congregational environments. Driven by genuine curiosity and love of learning, first-hand experiences in "new" sanctuaries and worship services, along with meeting "new" believers, opens the way for deeper understanding and insight.

Cooperative Religion may be the "highest level" on a relevant religious path, if there are levels or degrees. Holding this view assumes several critically important things: Competition is out, and an evolving, working knowledge of other views is valued.

The third "C"—*Cooperative*—is based on commonalities—common concerns handled with common sense. It's ultimately about cooperation, plain and simple.

Does belief still matter? It certainly might. Is it an

obstacle to relationships or collaborative action? It doesn't have to be.

When I managed cooperative housing for independent seniors, our ecumenical board was composed of women and men who were members of local congregations and some who had no affiliation. Some of the residents of the cooperative housing participated in nearby faith communities, and others did not. None of that mattered. Collaborative leadership and cooperation in the household are what mattered.

This is the way cooperative religion works. It is about *what works*. It is grounded and centered in a learning community that may be composed of a wide diversity of experiences and opinions. In a real sense, beliefs take a backseat to building a better household, neighborhood, community, country, and world.

Rabbi Heschel warns us not to forget that the "true sanctuary has no walls"[47]—a surprising image coming from a person of faith. But when we consider the title of his book, *God in Search of Man*, we see that he's flipping the narrative, expanding the definition of sanctuary, and maybe the definition of God. If humans spend their lives seeking the "spiritual" in big boxes of belief, they may have to rethink their sense of sanctuary as a limited space—protecting restricted beliefs—that can never hold the Limitless.

Secular people aren't waiting outside the walls for the

competitions and comparisons to play out. They're ready for fewer barriers and more cooperation.

Once we decide to progress along the path of the "Three C's," growing more accustomed to cooperative relationships, a "sanctuary without walls" may become a shared, welcoming space—religion or no religion.

Colors of Truth

One family Bible I used in my youthful evangelistic years had a zippered leather cover, gold-edged pages, and the words of Jesus in red. I still have the Bible I used in seminary, and it's a "red-letter edition" too. Flipping through the Four Gospels it's easy to see at a glance what Jesus actually said. You might say I've been "seeing red" for a long time.

Of course, no one knows what Jesus in fact said. We don't have even one original copy of those early writings. And if we did, we can be sure anything Jesus may have said wouldn't be in red, yellow, or green. We don't even have it in black.

Are we certain that the "Sermon on the Mount" was spoken by Jesus? Let's say that it was. Did someone record all those words? John chapter 17 is one long prayer Jesus spoke to his heavenly "Father." Was someone there to hear the prayer? If they were, why on earth would they write it down, and without a modern felt-tipped marker and a pocket pad, how would they do it? It also seems disrespectful to be writing while someone is praying.

I know the objections. Many Christians believe the scripture was "God-breathed" and that the Holy Spirit dictated each and every word directly to the writer of each verse. No one had to take dictation or even remember the words. The Spirit whispered the words later, and each word is exactly the way God meant it to be. Of course, not all Christians view the Bible this way.

As you thumb through the Gospels in a red-letter edition, there's a lot of black ink on the pages. It isn't all red. Someone, a narrator, is telling the story. We don't know exactly who wrote these stories, but the early Church put names on each collection: Matthew, Mark, Luke, and John. Thomas, Judas, and Mary's Gospels were voted out. As far as we know, Jesus never wrote one word, let alone one book. All we have are officially approved quotes.

This brings me to the "red-letter Christians." These are believers who try to live by the "actual words of Jesus" written in red in some editions of the Bible. I'm curious about these folks since most of the words in the Christian Scriptures—the "new" testament—are not in red. Red-letter believers give priority to "what Jesus said," which doesn't mean they don't believe the rest of the Bible. They just think Jesus' words are primary, central to a life of faith, and that it's nice to read a book where the best parts are already highlighted.

How are these Christians different from other Bible-believers? Well, they feel that the "heart of the Gospel" is found in the teachings of Jesus and not in Paul, Peter, James, John of Patmos, or any other assumed writer in the Bible. It simplifies things, but in a complicated way.

For instance, if a person doesn't turn to Paul and his theological speculations about Jesus or doesn't read the Bible much but simply goes along with the concepts taught over-and-over by trusted pastors and teachers, they are left with quite a different message than the red-letter-only message.

The Red-Letter Christians (RLC) website states, "Staying true to the foundation of combining Jesus and justice." They choose to "take Jesus seriously by endeavoring to live out His radical, counter-cultural teachings."

I saw that an RLC group held a revival at a location near Liberty University in Lynchburg, Virginia. The group took the position that the University is not being faithful to the red letters. One example: The University recently opened a *three-million-dollar gun range* on campus.

All this got me thinking: Do secular people have any "red-letter" writings? Are there "original sources" and teachings that could be viewed as the heart of our nonbelief?

Such writings wouldn't have to be written by atheists. Freethinkers or agnostics would do just fine too.

My mind goes to the wisdom of Thomas Paine, Frances Wright, Sojourner Truth, Ralph Waldo Emerson, Walt Whitman, and John Burroughs. I reflect on central texts from Robert Ingersoll, Elizabeth Cady Stanton, Lucretia Mott, Frederick Douglass, and others. In our time, I think of Carl Sagan, James Baldwin, Neil deGrasse Tyson, Stephen Hawking, Susan Jacoby, Ayaan Hirsi Ali, and many others.

What about ancient voices?   Plato, Socrates, Marcus Aurelius, and Hypatia.

Some might call these "Godless Gospels" but haven't all inspiring words, texts, and the teachers themselves been called "godless," "heretics," or "infidels" by someone?

Then there's the red-letter man himself, Jesus.   Could anything spoken by the world's most famous Palestinian Jewish apocalyptic prophet be in the Red-Letter Edition of the Secular Scriptures?

Consider: "Do not judge, so that you may not be judged,"[48] "Do to others as you would have them do to you,"[49] and "… you will know the truth, and the truth will make you free."[50] I would include one of my favorites, "Every good tree bears good fruit."[51] Let's not focus on what we believe, or don't believe.   Let's grow some healthy produce.

Whether it's from a "Godless Gospel" or "The Gospel," truth is truth.

Call me a rainbow-letter secular freethinker.

Healthier Choices

As I've often said, faith is a free choice, or ought to be. We hear of countries where people are treated badly, even imprisoned or killed, because they choose not to be a member of the "right religion." Across the globe, and maybe closer to home than we want to admit, people are shunned, excommunicated, bullied, or persecuted for making a decision not to hop aboard a particular theological train.

Freethought, sometimes disrespectfully called—"heresy" or "infidelity"—offers a long tradition of providing an ideological home to individuals who refuse to ride the "accepted" theological train. It began with the first human being who listened to a story, sermon, or scripture and walked out, or questioned, or simply stood up and stated, "Sorry, but I can no longer accept that. It makes no sense to me. I don't acknowledge your authority. I must go another way—my own way."

Notice this person—call him or her the first freethinker—was not as we say in the verbiage of today, "blasting," "slamming," "shaming," "taking down" or "throwing shade" on the others. He or she was merely expressing a personal view, her or his own thoughts and feelings as a reasonable individual.

When organizations or groups can't handle a freethinker or when a freethinker decides to leave instead of stay, we end up with revolution instead of reform. We get sectarianism instead of compromise. Instead of communication and collaboration, we are left with "sides" and orthodoxy (my opinion is right, yours is wrong).

Do you ever wonder what might have happened in history if Moses had held council with the Canaanites, if Buddha had sat with his Hindu neighbors, if Jesus had broken bread with the Pharisees, and if Muhammad had organized a conference with the Arabian leadership? If only they could have stayed in relationship with their former fellowships. And if only the leaders of their former groups could have listened with open minds. Think how much they all could have gained and learned, from each other— from honesty, sincerity, and respectful dialogue.

When I was managing several cooperative homes for independent seniors in the San Francisco Bay Area, an important component of my job was giving tours of each home to prospective residents and, if they were seriously interested in living there, conducting interviews.

I always made it clear that the "foundation" of each household was respect centered on cooperation and good communication. Many welcomed that. Some were honest to admit this model of co-housing wouldn't work for them. Unfortunately, others would verbally assent to our minimal rules of responsibility and later prove to be a poor match for renting a room with us. That could lead to an unhappy result for everyone involved.

With choice comes responsibility and with responsibility comes choice. Not every person can handle that, especially when living in close quarters with a diverse group of personalities, many set in their ways.

As a manager, I had the "joyful" job of being gatekeeper, peacekeeper, and too often, exit-maker. With extensive experience in compassionate "presence ministry," I couldn't help finding parallels with religion. How do we get folks to peacefully share a home, a neighborhood, a nation, or a planet? And who can, or will, or is crazy enough to manage such a task?

In the manager's office, I hung the famous quote by Martin Luther King, Jr.:

> This is the great new problem of mankind. We have inherited a large house, a great 'world house' in which we have to live together— black and white, Easterner and Westerner, Gentile and Jew, Catholic and Protestant, Moslem and Hindu—a family unduly separated in ideas, culture and interest, who, because we can never again live apart, must learn somehow to live with each other in

peace.[52]

I like my space and my way of living as much as anyone. Still, there have to be compromises—communal promises—and we have to "make room" in the great house of life for a central living room where relationships are central, where respect and responsibility are practiced. Otherwise, the household descends into division—chairs at the common table sit empty.

Residents of the senior homes I managed often found it challenging, to say the least, to agree on very basic things: the setting of the thermostat, cleanliness, chores, security issues, and of course, menus.

Our longsuffering Latino chef did everything he could to please folks with the meals he prepared, even when I assured him he would never please every resident. Still, he served a variety of dishes, and most people didn't grumble all that much.

Which, again, seats me back at the table of theology in the restaurant we call religion. If we look a little closer at what's offered, especially the "Specials," we may want to try new dishes, just for a fresh taste. If we find the menu limited, it may serve as an invitation to suggest a new menu or time to search for another restaurant.

The *divine deli* may not be what we're looking for. Maybe a potluck, something more open-air is what we need. A picnic on the bridge doesn't sound too bad does it?

Reader Response

If you liked this book, I encourage you to "give it some stars" on its Amazon sales page and spread the word on social media.

How are you repairing bridges or building community where you live?

I welcome your questions and comments. Feel free to contact me through my website: www.chighland.com.

I look forward to hearing from you. Thank you!

Chris Highland

Endnotes

1 Karen Strassler, "What We Lose When We Go From the Classroom to Zoom," *New York Times*, May 4, 2020.
https://www.nytimes.com/2020/05/04/sunday-review/zoom-college-classroom.html (accessed June 8, 2020).

2 William C. Shiel Jr., "Medical Definition of Gephyrophobia," MedicineNet,
https://www.medicinenet.com/script/main/art.asp?articlekey=12338. (accessed June 8, 2020).

3 Frederick Law Olmsted, *A Journey in the Seaboard Slave States, With Remarks on Their Economy*, (New York: Dix and Edwards, 1856), 133.

4 Frederick Douglass, "A Lecture on Slavery," Rochester, NY, December 1, 1850. *Frederick Douglass: Autobiographies*, ed. Henry Louis Gates Jr., (New York: Literary Classics of the United States, Inc., 1994), 419.

5 Frederick Douglass, "The Church and Prejudice," Plymouth, Massachusetts, November 4, 1841, *Great Speeches by Frederick Douglass*, (Mineola: Dover Publications, 2013), 1.

6 Frederick Douglass, *Great Speeches by Frederick Douglass*, 1-2.

7 Frederick Douglass, "Reception Speech," Finsbury Chapel,

Moorfields, England, May 22, 1846, *Frederick Douglass: Autobiographies*, 406.

[8] Frederick Douglass, "Reception Speech," Finsbury Chapel, Moorfields, England, May 22, 1846, *Frederick Douglass: Autobiographies*, 407.

[9] Bob Drury and Tom Clavin, *The Heart of Everything That Is*, (New York: Simon and Schuster, Inc., 2013), 11, 15.

[10] John Burroughs, *Wake-Robin*, (New York: Houghton, Mifflin and Company, 1902, originally published in 1871), 68.

[11] John Burroughs, 55, 47, 68.

[12] John Steinbeck, *The Grapes of Wrath*, (New York: Penguin Books, 1976, originally published, 1939), 321.

[13] John Steinbeck, 280-281.

[14] Numbers 6:24, NRSV.

[15] Luke 6:20, NRSV.

[16] Psalm 115:15, NRSV.

[17] Luke 1:42, NRSV.

[18] Qur'an, 11:73.

[19] Mary Oliver, "The Summer Day" in *New and Selected Poems*, (Boston: Beacon Press, 1992), 94.

[20] Roy Morris, Jr., *The Better Angel: Walt Whitman in the Civil War*, (New York: Oxford University Press, Inc., 2000), 7.

[21] Hebrews 13:2, NRSV.

[22] Marcus Aurelius, *The Meditations of Marcus Aurelius*, tr. George Long, (New York: P.F. Collier and Son, 1909, Harvard Classics), selections.

[23] Marcus Aurelius.

[24] Marcus Aurelius.

[25] Marcus Aurelius.

[26] Marcus Aurelius.

[27] Terry Tempest Williams, *The Hour of Land*, (New York: Picador,

2016), 216.

[28] Terry Tempest Williams, 216.

[29] Terry Tempest Williams, 217-218.

[30] "After an unsuccessful revolt following the arrival of Chinese troops in Tibet, the Dalai fled Lhasa in fear for his life. Only 23 years old, he and his followers crossed a treacherous Himalayan pass into India on horseback, arriving on March 31, 1959." Source: CNN website, https://www.cnn.com/2019/03/30/asia/dalai-lama-tibet-china-intl/index.html, accessed May 21, 2020.

[31] The Dalai Lama, *Beyond Religion*, (New York: Houghton Mifflin Harcourt Publishing Co., 2011), 22.

[32] The Dalai Lama, 17-18.

[33] The Dalai Lama, 19.

[34] The Dalai Lama, 48.

[35] The Dalai Lama, 112-113.

[36] The Dalai Lama, 104-105.

[37] The Dalai Lama, 107.

[38] *The Apple Dictionary*.

[39] *The Apple Dictionary*.

[40] 1 Peter 5:8, NRSV.

[41] James 4:7, NRSV.

[42] James 4:11, NRSV.

[43] *The Apple Dictionary*.

[44] *The Apple Dictionary*.

[45] Leo Booth, *When God Becomes a Drug: Breaking the Chains of Religious Addiction and Abuse*, now titled, *When God Becomes a Drug: Book 1; Understanding Religious Addiction and Religious Abuse*, (England: SCP Limited, 1998). The quote is taken from the book description on Amazon: https://www.amazon.com/gp/product/0962328294/ref=dbs_a_def_rw t_bibl_vppi_i3.

[46] Abraham Joshua Heschel, *God in Search of Man*, (New York, Farrar, Straus and Giroux, 1955), Kindle Edition.

[47] Abraham Joshua Heschel, Kindle Edition.

[48] Matthew 7:1, NRSV.

[49] Luke 6:31, NRSV.

[50] John 8:32, NRSV.

[51] Matthew 7:17 NRSV.

[52] Martin Luther King, Jr., ed. James M. Washington, "Where Do We Go From Here?," *A Testament of Hope: The Essential Writings and Speeches of Martin Luther King, Jr.*, (San Francisco: Harper Collins, 1986), 617.

Made in the USA
San Bernardino, CA
29 June 2020